Career Compass

Navigating the Path to Professional Success

By

Dr. David K. Ewen

Professor / Entrepreneur

ISBN: 9798882721939
Imprint: Independently published by Enterprise College

Cover art by Warren via Unsplash

About the Book

Embark on a transformative journey of self-discovery and career development with "Career Compass: Navigating the Path to Professional Success". Learn to identify your strengths and passions, laying the foundation for a fulfilling career path. Discover the power of presenting yourself authentically and effectively to the world. Explore various career paths and industries, equipped with the tools to build a standout resume. Harness the power of networking and master the intricacies of job searching. Prepare to shine in interviews and negotiate your worth confidently. Unlock strategies for continuous professional growth and leverage online platforms for career success. Learn to overcome obstacles and setbacks, paving the way for sustained career excellence. With practical advice and actionable insights, this guide empowers you to navigate your career journey with clarity, confidence, and purpose.

Dr. David K. Ewen

About the Author

Dr. David K. Ewen, a seasoned entrepreneur since 1994 and esteemed professor since 2004, has dedicated his career to empowering individuals in their pursuit of success. With decades of experience in both academia and business, Dr. Ewen has been instrumental in guiding countless individuals towards achieving their professional goals. Through his expertise, mentorship, and dedication, he has played a pivotal role in helping people develop the skills, knowledge, and strategies necessary for building thriving careers.

Table of Contents

Chapter 1: Assessing Your Skills and Interests

Assessing your skills and interests is not just a preliminary step but a foundational pillar in shaping your career path and personal development journey. It's akin to navigating with a map; without understanding your starting point and destination, you're more likely to wander aimlessly. By investing the time to thoroughly evaluate your aptitudes and passions, you equip yourself with invaluable insights that can steer your decisions towards paths that truly resonate with who you are and what you aim to achieve.

First and foremost, reflecting on your skills involves a deep dive into understanding your strengths, weaknesses, and areas with potential for improvement. This introspective process fosters self-awareness, a cornerstone of personal growth. Recognizing your strengths allows you to leverage them effectively, maximizing your potential in areas where you excel. Simultaneously, acknowledging your weaknesses provides clarity on where to direct your efforts for skill enhancement. This self-awareness not only empowers you to play to your strengths but also motivates you to continuously strive for improvement, fostering a mindset of lifelong learning and development.

Similarly, exploring your interests is essential for uncovering what truly ignites your passion and enthusiasm. Identifying activities, subjects, or causes that genuinely captivate your interest provides valuable clues about potential career paths or areas of focus. When you align your skills with your interests, you create a synergy that propels you towards meaningful and fulfilling endeavors. Passion is a powerful driver; it fuels persistence, creativity, and resilience, making challenges seem more like opportunities for growth rather than obstacles to overcome.

Moreover, assessing your skills and interests opens up new vistas of opportunities for growth and exploration. It encourages you to step out of your comfort zone, try new experiences, and venture into uncharted territories. This adventurous spirit not only broadens your horizons but also exposes you to diverse perspectives and possibilities. Embracing this mindset of exploration and discovery can lead you to unexpected pathways that resonate more deeply with your authentic self.

Ultimately, the process of assessing your skills and interests is not just about charting a career path but about crafting a life that aligns with your values, passions, and aspirations. It empowers you to make intentional choices that nurture your personal and professional fulfillment, leading to a more purposeful and meaningful journey. So, embrace the journey of self-discovery, for within it lies the key to unlocking your fullest potential and living a life rich in fulfillment and purpose.

Chapter 2: Crafting Your Personal Brand

Crafting your personal brand is akin to sculpting a masterpiece; it's about defining and refining the essence of who you are and how you wish to be perceived by the world. In today's interconnected landscape, where impressions are formed within seconds and information is readily accessible, your personal brand serves as a compass guiding your interactions, opportunities, and relationships.

At its core, your personal brand encapsulates your unique blend of strengths, values, skills, and personality traits. It's the story you tell through your actions, words, and appearance—a narrative that distinguishes you from the crowd and leaves a lasting impression. Developing a strong personal brand requires a foundation of self-awareness, where you introspectively examine your passions, strengths, and aspirations. By understanding what sets you apart, you can strategically position yourself in a way that resonates with your target audience.

Consistency is key in building and maintaining your personal brand. Whether online or offline, every interaction serves as a building block in shaping perceptions. From the content you share on social media to the way you present yourself in professional settings, maintaining a cohesive image reinforces authenticity and credibility. Authenticity, in particular, is the cornerstone of a compelling personal brand. It's about staying true to your values, beliefs, and personality, even in the face of external pressures or trends. Authenticity breeds trust and fosters genuine connections, which are invaluable assets in both personal and professional realms.

In today's digital age, establishing a professional online presence is paramount. Social media platforms, personal websites, and professional networking sites offer avenues to showcase your expertise, share your insights, and engage with like-minded individuals. By curating content that aligns with your personal brand, you not only amplify your reach but also attract opportunities that align with your goals and values.

However, personal branding isn't solely confined to the digital realm. Offline interactions, such as networking events, conferences, and face-to-face meetings, are equally vital in shaping perceptions and building meaningful connections. Every encounter is an opportunity to reinforce your personal brand through your demeanor, communication style, and interpersonal skills.

Ultimately, crafting your personal brand is an ongoing journey of self-discovery, refinement, and communication. It requires introspection, consistency, and a willingness to evolve with changing circumstances. By defining and embodying your personal brand, you not only stand out in a crowded world but also leave a lasting impact on those you encounter. So, embrace the process, harness your uniqueness, and let your personal brand illuminate your path to success and fulfillment.

Chapter 3: Exploring Career Paths and Industries

Exploring career paths and industries is akin to embarking on a voyage of self-discovery and professional growth. In today's dynamic world, where opportunities abound and industries evolve rapidly, individuals have the privilege to chart their own course and discover where their passions truly lie. This journey of exploration is not just about finding a job; it's about uncovering a vocation that resonates with one's values, interests, and aspirations.

Research serves as the compass in this journey, offering valuable insights into the multitude of career paths and industries available. Through diligent investigation, individuals can gain a deeper understanding of different fields, including their requirements, opportunities, and potential for growth. Whether through online resources, informational interviews, or industry reports, research provides a solid foundation for informed decision-making.

Networking plays a pivotal role in the exploration process, offering opportunities to connect with professionals across various industries. Engaging in networking events, industry conferences, and online communities allows individuals to glean firsthand perspectives and advice from those who have traversed similar paths. Mentorship, in particular, provides invaluable guidance and support, offering insights into the nuances of different industries and career trajectories.

Internships and experiential learning opportunities offer a hands-on approach to exploring career paths, allowing individuals to immerse themselves in different roles and environments. These experiences not only provide practical skills and knowledge but also offer a glimpse into the day-to-day realities of various professions. From internships to volunteer work, each opportunity serves as a stepping stone in the journey of exploration, helping individuals refine their interests and goals.

By embracing this journey of exploration, individuals not only broaden their horizons but also cultivate a diverse skill set and perspective. Exposure to different industries fosters adaptability and resilience, empowering individuals to thrive in an ever-changing job market. Moreover, understanding the intricacies of various industries enables individuals to make strategic career decisions, positioning themselves for long-term success and fulfillment.

Ultimately, exploring career paths and industries is a transformative process that empowers individuals to navigate their professional lives with confidence and clarity. It's about embracing curiosity, seizing opportunities, and forging a path that aligns with one's passions and aspirations. Through research, networking, and hands-on experiences, individuals can unlock a world of possibilities, discovering not just a job, but a meaningful and fulfilling career.

Chapter 4: Building a Winning Resume

Crafting a winning resume is akin to creating a compelling advertisement for oneself in the job market—a concise yet comprehensive document that highlights one's unique qualifications, experiences, and accomplishments. In today's competitive landscape, a well-crafted resume is often the first impression a candidate makes on a potential employer, making it a crucial tool in securing job opportunities and advancing in one's career.

To build an effective resume, organization and clarity are paramount. Information should be presented in a structured format, with clear headings, bullet points, and concise language to ensure readability and comprehension. A clutter-free layout allows recruiters to quickly identify key details and relevant information, saving time and facilitating a positive impression.

Tailoring the resume to the specific job being applied for is essential. This involves customizing the content to highlight relevant experiences, skills, and achievements that directly align with the job requirements and company culture. By demonstrating a clear understanding of the role and showcasing how one's background and capabilities meet the employer's needs, candidates can significantly increase their chances of standing out among other applicants.

Including quantifiable achievements and results adds credibility and impact to the resume. Metrics, such as sales figures, project outcomes, or performance improvements, provide tangible evidence of one's contributions and effectiveness in previous roles. These achievements not only showcase capabilities but also illustrate the potential value the candidate can bring to the prospective employer.

Moreover, incorporating keywords from the job description is crucial, especially when applying online. Many companies use applicant tracking systems (ATS) to screen resumes for relevant keywords and phrases. By strategically integrating these keywords into the resume, candidates can improve their chances of passing through the initial screening process and getting noticed by hiring managers.

A winning resume should also adhere to professional standards in terms of format, grammar, and design. It should be error-free, with attention to detail in spelling, punctuation, and grammar. Additionally, a clean and visually appealing design enhances readability and creates a positive impression. Simple formatting, consistent font usage, and ample white space contribute to a polished and professional appearance.

In conclusion, investing time and effort into building a winning resume can significantly enhance one's chances of securing job interviews and advancing in their career. By organizing information effectively, tailoring content to the job at hand, showcasing quantifiable achievements, and adhering to professional standards, candidates can create a compelling document that effectively communicates their value proposition to potential employers.

Chapter 5: Mastering the Art of Networking

Mastering the art of networking is akin to unlocking a treasure trove of opportunities and connections that can propel one's personal and professional growth to new heights. It transcends mere socializing; it's about cultivating meaningful relationships built on trust, reciprocity, and genuine interest in others. In today's interconnected world, where success often hinges on who you know as much as what you know, mastering the art of networking is essential for navigating the complexities of modern life.

At the heart of effective networking lies the ability to listen actively and communicate clearly. By showing genuine interest in others' experiences, perspectives, and aspirations, individuals can forge authentic connections that go beyond surface-level interactions.

Whether at networking events, professional conferences, or online communities, actively engaging with others fosters rapport and lays the foundation for lasting relationships.

Networking is not just about expanding one's circle of contacts; it's about leveraging those connections to mutual benefit. By offering support, insights, or assistance to others, individuals can add value to their relationships and cultivate goodwill within their network. Likewise, being open to receiving help, advice, or opportunities from others fosters a culture of reciprocity and collaboration, where everyone can thrive and succeed together.

Attending networking events and joining professional organizations provide valuable opportunities to expand one's network and tap into a diverse pool of talents and resources. Whether seeking career advice, mentorship, or potential collaborators, these platforms offer a wealth of knowledge and expertise waiting to be tapped into. Additionally, engaging in online communities and social media groups enables individuals to connect with like-minded individuals from around the globe, transcending geographical boundaries and fostering a sense of belonging in a digital age.

Moreover, networking is not just a means to advance one's career; it's also a catalyst for personal growth and development. By surrounding oneself with individuals who inspire, challenge, and support, individuals can glean valuable insights, broaden their perspectives, and push beyond their comfort zones. Mentorship, in particular, plays a crucial role in this process, offering guidance, wisdom, and encouragement as individuals navigate their professional journeys.

Ultimately, mastering the art of networking is a lifelong skill that requires patience, perseverance, and authenticity. It's about building a strong foundation of relationships that can weather the test of time and circumstances. By investing in meaningful connections, adding value to others, and staying open to new opportunities, individuals can unlock a world of possibilities and enriching experiences in both their personal and professional lives. So, embrace the power of networking, and watch as doors of opportunity swing open before you, leading to a future filled with success, fulfillment, and meaningful connections.

Chapter 6: Navigating the Job Search Landscape

Navigating the job search landscape can feel like traversing uncharted territory, especially in today's competitive market. However, with a strategic approach and proactive mindset, individuals can successfully navigate this journey and secure rewarding employment opportunities that align with their career aspirations.

The first step in the job search process is self-assessment. Understanding your strengths, skills, and interests is crucial in identifying the types of roles that are a good fit for you. Take the time to reflect on your past experiences, achievements, and career goals to gain clarity on your professional direction.

Researching potential employers and industries can help you narrow down your job search and target companies that align with your values and aspirations. Explore company websites, industry reports, and professional networks to gather insights into organizational culture, values, and career opportunities.

Building a strong professional network is another key aspect of the job search process. Platforms like LinkedIn offer valuable opportunities to connect with professionals in your field, attend networking events, and reach out to industry contacts for informational interviews. Networking can uncover hidden job opportunities and provide valuable insights into the job market.

Crafting a tailored resume and cover letter for each application is essential in making a positive impression on hiring managers.

Highlight your relevant experiences, skills, and achievements that demonstrate your qualifications for the role. Tailoring your application materials shows your genuine interest in the position and increases your chances of standing out among other applicants.

Utilizing various job search channels, such as online job boards, career fairs, recruitment agencies, and social media platforms, can expand your job search reach and increase your chances of finding relevant opportunities. Be proactive in seeking out opportunities and stay organized in tracking your applications and follow-ups.

Preparing for job interviews is crucial in showcasing your qualifications and enthusiasm for the role. Practice common interview questions, research the company and industry, and be prepared to articulate how your skills and experiences align with the role's requirements. Demonstrate your passion, professionalism, and readiness to contribute to the organization's success.

Approaching the job search process with determination, resilience, and a proactive mindset is key to navigating the job search landscape effectively. Stay focused on your goals, leverage your strengths and network, and remain open to new opportunities and experiences. With persistence and dedication, you can secure fulfilling employment opportunities that propel your career forward.

Chapter 7: Rocking the Interview Process

Rocking the interview process is not just about answering questions; it's about showcasing your skills, personality, and enthusiasm in a way that leaves a lasting impression on potential employers. Preparation is key to success, and it begins long before you walk into the interview room.

Start by thoroughly researching the company and understanding the job role. Familiarize yourself with the company's mission, values, recent news, and any notable projects or initiatives. This knowledge demonstrates your genuine interest in the organization and allows you to tailor your responses to align with its goals and culture. Similarly, understanding the job requirements and responsibilities enables you to articulate how your skills and experiences make you a perfect fit for the role.

Practice common interview questions, both behavioral and technical, to build confidence and refine your responses. Consider conducting mock interviews with friends or mentors to receive feedback and fine-tune your communication skills. Additionally, prepare specific examples from your past experiences that highlight your achievements, problem-solving abilities, and contributions to previous roles.

On the day of the interview, arrive early, well-dressed, and composed. Punctuality and professionalism demonstrate respect for the interviewer's time and reflect positively on your reliability and commitment. Throughout the interview, maintain eye contact, speak clearly and confidently, and engage with the interviewer by asking questions and actively listening to their responses.

When answering questions, focus on highlighting your relevant skills, experiences, and accomplishments. Use specific examples to illustrate your capabilities and demonstrate how you have successfully tackled challenges or achieved results in the past. Be honest and authentic in your responses, showcasing your personality and enthusiasm for the position.

Asking thoughtful questions about the company culture, team dynamics, and future opportunities not only demonstrates your interest and engagement but also provides valuable insights into whether the role is the right fit for you. Remember, interviews are a two-way street, and it's essential to assess whether the company aligns with your values and career goals as well.

After the interview, send a personalized thank-you email to express your gratitude for the opportunity and reiterate your interest in the position. This gesture demonstrates professionalism and leaves a positive impression on the interviewer, potentially tipping the scales in your favor.

By approaching the interview process with confidence, preparation, and professionalism, you can maximize your chances of success and stand out among other applicants. Remember to be yourself, showcase your strengths, and let your passion for the role shine through. With the right mindset and preparation, you can rock the interview and secure the job opportunity you've been working towards.

Chapter 8: Negotiating Your Salary and Benefits Package

Negotiating your salary and benefits package is a pivotal aspect of the job-seeking process, wielding significant influence over your financial stability and overall job satisfaction. Approaching this stage with preparation, clarity, and a collaborative mindset can make a substantial difference in securing terms that align with your worth and needs.

First and foremost, thorough research is paramount. Understanding industry standards, the financial health of the company, and the cost of living in the area provides essential context for negotiations. Armed with this knowledge, you can establish a reasonable range for salary and benefits expectations, ensuring that your requests are both fair and realistic.

When delving into salary discussions, it's crucial to consider the entirety of the compensation package. While base pay is important, additional perks such as bonuses, stock options, paid time off, retirement contributions, and healthcare benefits can significantly enhance your overall compensation. Evaluating the total value of the package allows for a more comprehensive assessment of its worth to you.

Effectively articulating your value to the company is key to successful negotiations. Highlighting your relevant experience, skills, and achievements demonstrates the unique contributions you bring to the table. Providing concrete examples of how your abilities have positively impacted previous employers can bolster your case and justify your desired compensation.

Approaching negotiations with a positive and collaborative mindset sets the stage for a constructive dialogue. Instead of viewing it as a confrontational exchange, strive for a win-win outcome where both parties feel satisfied with the final agreement. Emphasize your interest in building a mutually beneficial relationship with the company, fostering goodwill and rapport throughout the process.

It's important to remember that negotiating your salary is not just a one-time event but an ongoing process that can shape your earning potential and career trajectory in the long term. Regularly reassessing your compensation in light of changing circumstances, market trends, and personal achievements ensures that you are fairly compensated for your contributions and valued as a vital asset to the organization.

In conclusion, negotiating your salary and benefits package requires careful preparation, effective communication, and a collaborative approach. By conducting thorough research, articulating your value, and fostering a positive dialogue with the employer, you can secure terms that reflect your worth and set the stage for a successful and fulfilling career journey.

Chapter 9: Developing Professional Growth Strategies

Developing professional growth strategies is akin to charting a course towards success in one's career journey. It involves deliberate planning, self-assessment, continuous learning, and proactive engagement with opportunities for advancement. By implementing effective strategies, individuals can enhance their skills, expand their networks, and achieve their long-term career aspirations.

Setting clear and achievable objectives is foundational to professional growth. This begins with a thorough self-assessment to identify strengths, weaknesses, and areas for improvement. By understanding one's current standing, individuals can develop targeted goals that align with their career aspirations.

These objectives serve as a roadmap, guiding individuals towards milestones and achievements that contribute to their professional development.

Networking is a critical component of professional growth strategies. Building relationships with mentors, peers, and industry professionals can provide valuable insights, guidance, and opportunities for growth. Networking opportunities abound in professional associations, industry events, and online communities, offering avenues for collaboration, mentorship, and career advancement.

Continuous learning is essential for remaining competitive in today's fast-paced job market. Whether through formal education, online courses, workshops, or conferences, investing in ongoing learning and skill development is paramount. Staying updated with the latest industry trends, technological advancements, and best practices ensures relevance and adaptability in a rapidly evolving landscape.

Seeking feedback from supervisors, colleagues, and clients is another crucial aspect of professional growth. Constructive feedback offers valuable perspectives on one's performance, strengths, and areas for development. Embracing feedback with an open mind and a willingness to learn fosters self-awareness and personal growth, ultimately contributing to professional success.

Embracing challenges and stepping out of one's comfort zone are essential for personal and professional growth. Taking on new responsibilities, pursuing stretch assignments, and tackling unfamiliar tasks cultivates resilience, adaptability, and confidence. Embracing a growth mindset allows individuals to view challenges as opportunities for learning and development, propelling them towards greater achievements.

In conclusion, developing professional growth strategies requires a proactive and intentional approach. By setting clear objectives, building networks, investing in continuous learning, seeking feedback, and embracing challenges, individuals can navigate their career paths successfully and achieve their professional goals. With determination, resilience, and a commitment to growth, individuals can unlock their full potential and thrive in their chosen fields.

Chapter 10: Leveraging Online Platforms and Resources

In today's digital age, harnessing the power of online platforms and resources has become indispensable for individuals navigating the complexities of career search, development, and growth. With a plethora of tools and platforms available at their fingertips, individuals now have unprecedented access to opportunities, knowledge, and connections that can propel their professional journeys forward.

Platforms like LinkedIn have emerged as virtual hubs for networking, job hunting, and personal branding. Here, individuals can showcase their qualifications, connect with professionals in their field of interest, and engage with potential employers. By curating a compelling profile and actively participating in relevant groups and discussions, users can expand their professional network and discover new career opportunities.

Online learning platforms such as Coursera, Udemy, and Khan Academy have democratized education, offering a wealth of courses and tutorials covering a broad spectrum of topics. Whether individuals seek to acquire new skills, deepen their expertise in a particular area, or explore new career paths, these platforms provide flexible and accessible learning opportunities. From technical skills like coding and data analysis to soft skills like leadership and communication, the possibilities for continuous learning are virtually endless.

Moreover, job search websites like Indeed, Glassdoor, and Monster have revolutionized the way individuals search for employment opportunities. These platforms allow users to browse job listings, research companies, and access valuable insights from current and former employees. By reading reviews, salary information, and company profiles, individuals can make more informed decisions about their career paths and potential employers, ensuring a better fit for their skills, values, and aspirations.

By leveraging these online platforms and resources effectively, individuals can not only find job opportunities that align with their career goals but also continuously develop and grow in their chosen field. Whether by expanding their professional network, acquiring new skills, or researching potential employers, the digital landscape offers a wealth of opportunities for career advancement and personal fulfillment. In today's rapidly evolving job market, embracing the power of online platforms is essential for staying competitive, adaptable, and successful in one's professional endeavors.

Chapter 11: Overcoming Career Challenges and Setbacks

Navigating the twists and turns of a professional journey often entails encountering career challenges and setbacks. Whether it's facing job loss, rejection, failure, or burnout, these hurdles can be disheartening. However, it's crucial to recognize that setbacks are not permanent roadblocks; rather, they present opportunities for growth and resilience.

Maintaining a positive mindset and perspective is paramount when overcoming career challenges. Viewing setbacks as learning experiences fosters a sense of determination and perseverance. By reframing setbacks as stepping stones to personal and professional development, individuals can cultivate resilience and find the motivation to press forward despite adversity.

Seeking support from mentors, colleagues, or career coaches can provide valuable insights and guidance during challenging times. Drawing upon the wisdom and experiences of others can offer fresh perspectives and practical strategies for overcoming obstacles. Additionally, surrounding oneself with a supportive network can provide emotional encouragement and motivation to stay resilient in the face of adversity.

Taking proactive steps is essential in overcoming career challenges and setbacks. Upskilling through education and training, networking to expand opportunities and connections, or exploring new career paths can all help individuals navigate through tough times and emerge stronger on the other side.

Embracing change, staying adaptable, and remaining true to one's goals and values are essential traits that enable individuals to overcome obstacles with resilience and confidence.

Ultimately, overcoming career challenges is not just about bouncing back; it's about bouncing forward. By embracing setbacks as opportunities for growth, seeking support from others, and taking proactive steps towards personal and professional development, individuals can emerge from adversity stronger, wiser, and more resilient than before. With determination, perseverance, and a positive mindset, individuals can navigate through career challenges and setbacks, ultimately achieving personal and professional growth.

Chapter 12: Sustaining Long-Term Career Success

Sustaining long-term career success is a dynamic and multifaceted journey that demands a blend of dedication, adaptability, and ongoing learning. Achieving enduring success in one's career requires more than just talent or luck; it necessitates a strong work ethic, perseverance, and a steadfast commitment to personal growth.

Setting clear goals and developing a strategic plan for career advancement is foundational to sustained success. By outlining specific objectives and mapping out actionable steps to achieve them, individuals can stay focused and motivated on their path to success. However, it's essential to remain flexible and open to adjusting these plans as circumstances and priorities evolve over time.

Building a robust professional network, cultivating relationships, and seeking mentorship are indispensable components of long-term success in any field. Connecting with peers, mentors, and industry leaders provides invaluable opportunities for collaboration, learning, and professional development. These relationships can offer guidance, support, and access to new opportunities throughout one's career journey.

Staying informed about industry trends, acquiring new skills, and embracing technological advancements are essential for remaining competitive and relevant in today's fast-paced job market. Continuous learning and skill development ensure that individuals can adapt to evolving demands and seize emerging opportunities in their field.

Balancing work-life commitments, prioritizing self-care, and fostering a healthy work environment are also vital aspects of sustaining long-term career success. Recognizing the importance of maintaining a sense of well-being and fulfillment outside of work contributes to overall job satisfaction and productivity.

Moreover, staying resilient in the face of challenges and setbacks is crucial for navigating the inevitable ups and downs of a career. Maintaining a positive attitude, learning from failures, and bouncing back stronger builds the resilience needed to overcome obstacles and persevere on the path to success.

In conclusion, sustaining long-term career success requires a holistic approach that encompasses goal-setting, networking, continuous learning, self-care, and resilience. By investing in personal and professional growth, cultivating meaningful relationships, and staying adaptable in the face of change, individuals can navigate their career paths with confidence and achieve lasting fulfillment and prosperity.

Dr. David K. Ewen

Career Compass

Navigating the Path to Professional Success

By

Dr. David K. Ewen

Professor / Entrepreneur